Contents

CPSIA information can be obtained
at www.ICGtesting.com
Printed in the USA
LVHW070043020420
651901LV00001B/2

9781925991994